D0845678

www.mascotbooks.com

How the People Trumped Ronald Plump

©2018 Brian and Ed Krassenstein. All Rights Reserved. No part of this publication may be reproduced, stored in a retrieval system or transmitted in any form by any means electronic, mechanical, or photocopying, recording or otherwise without the permission of the author.

This book is a parody that may provide false information, written for entertainment purposes only. The views and opinions expressed in this book are solely those of the author. These views and opinions do not necessarily represent those of the publisher or staff.

For more information, please contact:
Mascot Books
620 Herndon Parkway, Suite 320
Herndon, VA 20170
info@mascotbooks.com

Second printing. This Mascot Books edition printed in 2018

Library of Congress Control Number: 2018905103

CPSIA Code: PRTWP0618B
ISBN-13: 978-1-64307-076-6

Printed in Malaysia

How the People Trumped

RONALD PLUMP

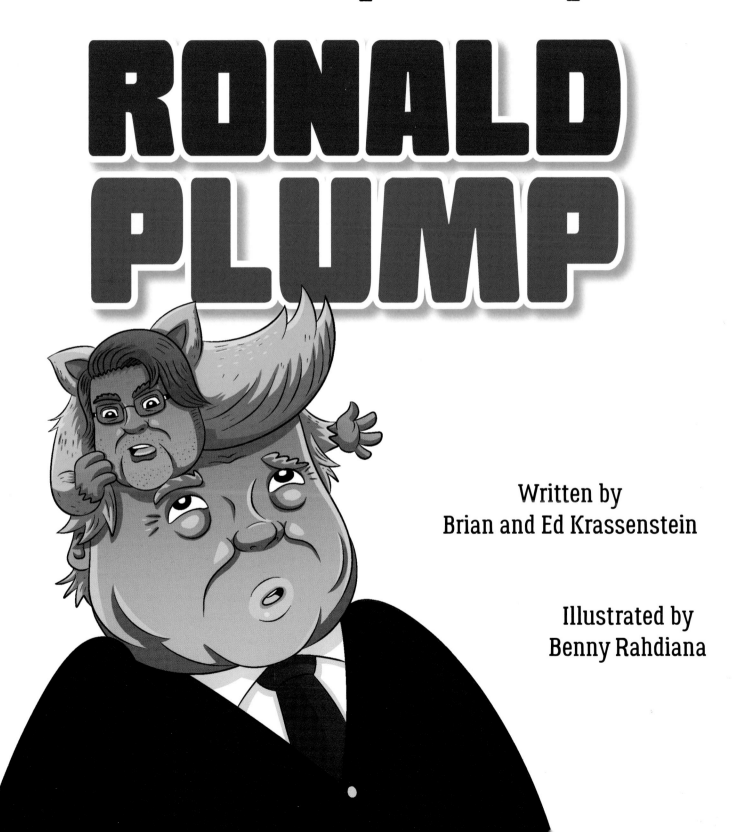

Written by
Brian and Ed Krassenstein

Illustrated by
Benny Rahdiana

In a bustling town called "Do Work City,"
There lived a man who was not very witty.
"RONALD PLUMP" was his notorious name,
And in a tower he resided in fame.

This man, he spoke loudly and carried a tiny stick,
With hands that had fingers as small as a candle's wick!
It's hard to imagine a man like **PLUMP**,
Filled with loneliness from becoming a miserable chump.

When one glanced upon the lonely **RONALD PLUMP**,
One thing stood out, and that was the clump.
The clump was of fur, and a brilliant gold.
It sat on his head like a custom-made mold.

The fur on his head was actually a squirrel,
A creature who wanted to rule the whole world.
Named "Weave Bannon," the squirrel would say,
All kinds of things that could ruin one's day.
Mr. **PLUMP** would listen, as he had no other friends,
And he wanted to impress Weave Bannon to no end.

Weave Bannon's thoughts were now in **PLUMP'S** head,
And **PLUMP** would adhere to every word that he said.
The evil little squirrel was now in command,
As **PLUMP** became a slave to every demand.

One blustery winter night the two of them planned,
"We must rule this town with a tiny, heavy hand.
We will make 'Do Work City' great again,
At the expense of all women and men."

Together they plotted with "Loudimir Tootin,"
"We must win this election, even if it means collusion."
Tootin was an evil man from many miles away,
But Bannon and **PLUMP** made a plan and put it underway.

By lying and cheating **PLUMP** shot to the top,
Hit the top of the polls, and then came the shock.
PLUMP was elected Leader of the town,
But most citizens saw him as a clown.
Although he won, he felt empty inside.
Cheating is bad and he was unqualified.

His very first action was to bring his family along.
Many questioned **PLUMP**, who thought nothing could go wrong.
"Ivannabe **PLUMP**" and "Jared Nepotism" joined the administration,
And this of course sparked much speculation.
PLUMP was using his power and fame,
To enrich his family with not a sign of shame.
Selfishness is no trait of a man who wants to lead,
Instead it's a characteristic of a man filled with greed.

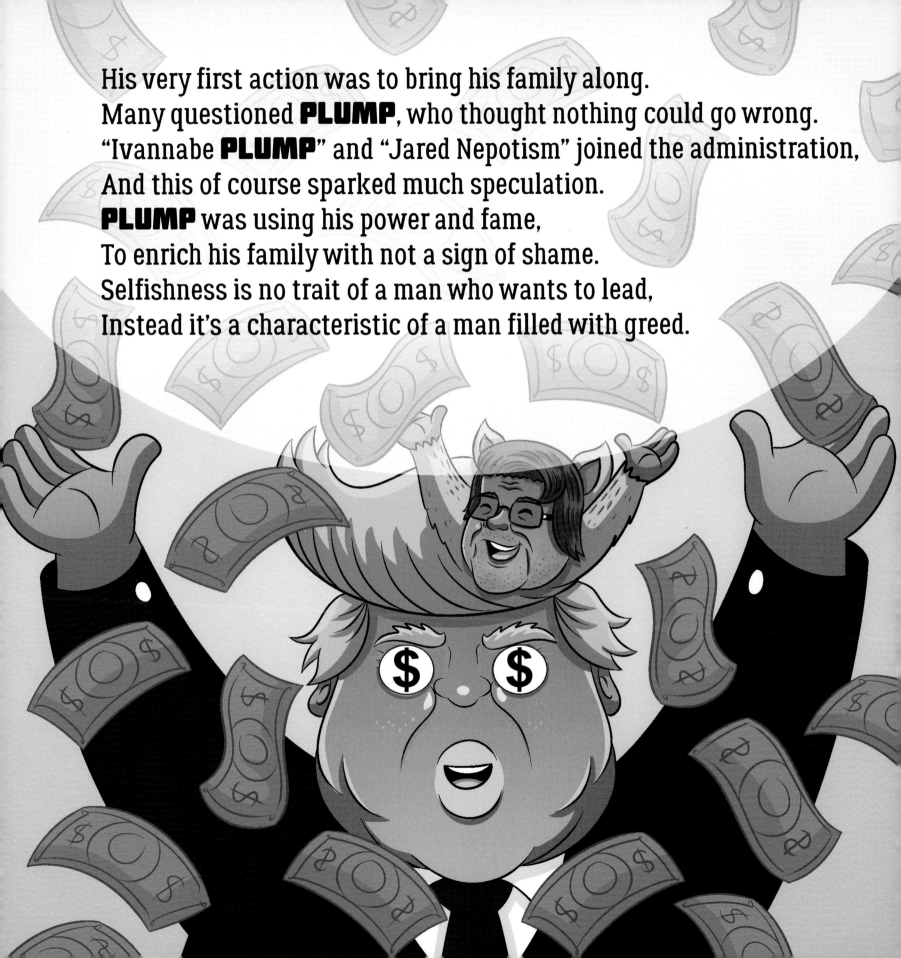

PLUMP wanted for the different to be banned,
He wanted to remove every not-like-him woman and man.
To take them from the town they loved and treasured,
For being different as only he measured.

The townspeople responded, sounding sad,
"Discrimination is hate, and hate is bad!
We are all the same, but believe different things,
Like how we got here and what peace really means."

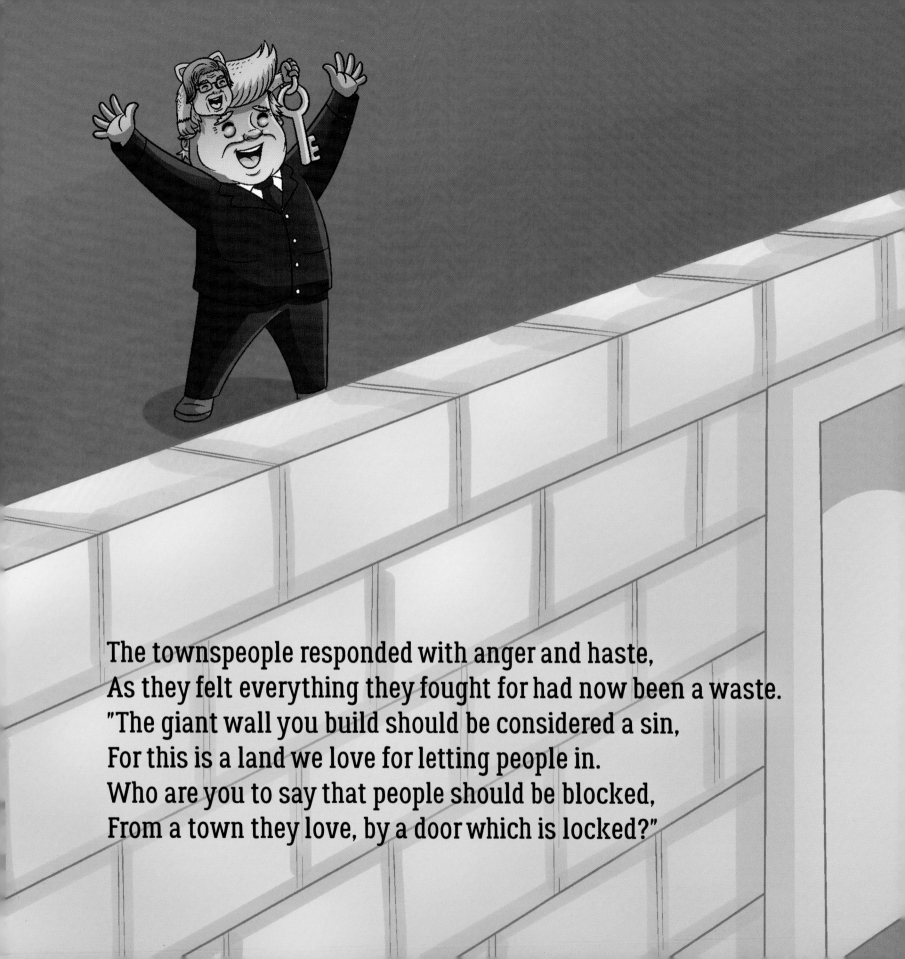

The townspeople responded with anger and haste,
As they felt everything they fought for had now been a waste.
"The giant wall you build should be considered a sin,
For this is a land we love for letting people in.
Who are you to say that people should be blocked,
From a town they love, by a door which is locked?"

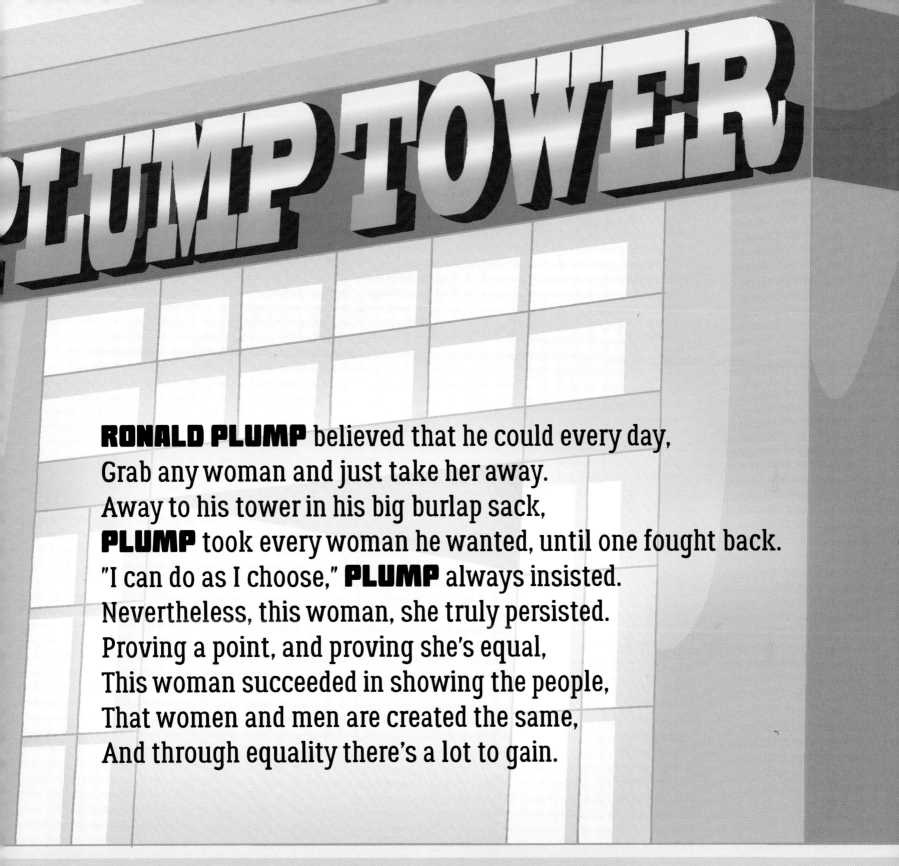

RONALD PLUMP believed that he could every day,
Grab any woman and just take her away.
Away to his tower in his big burlap sack,
PLUMP took every woman he wanted, until one fought back.
"I can do as I choose," **PLUMP** always insisted.
Nevertheless, this woman, she truly persisted.
Proving a point, and proving she's equal,
This woman succeeded in showing the people,
That women and men are created the same,
And through equality there's a lot to gain.

"The Resistance" was formed as the people fought back:
"We're all equal and **PLUMP'S** ideas are whack!"
PLUMP told lie after lie to the great people he led,
And after a while, no one believed a word that he said.
A boy who cries wolf becomes a man who misleads,
So the people no longer believed his lying misdeeds.

Lying is bad, lying is wrong,
It certainly isn't a trait of the strong.
But strong was not he, a man being controlled,
A story that simply cannot go untold.
A puppet of Tootin, a puppet of Bannon,
RONALD PLUMP had become a loose cannon.

Instead of fists, weapons, and rage,
The Resistance hatched a clever plan backstage.
"We'll use logic, sense, and reason," one said,
"To confuse the squirrel and remove him from **PLUMP'S** head."

Little by little that logic crept in,
Until Weave Bannon could no longer win.
Bannon's squirrely thoughts left **PLUMP'S** head in a flurry,
And the people's ideas were reborn in a hurry.

The story ends here for the famous Weave Bannon.
PLUMP no longer takes orders from that hateful loose cannon.
It's important to realize one should follow their heart,
Not abandon their morals to those who aren't smart.
A true leader is one filled with compassion.
PLUMP and his ideas are now out of fashion.

Bald and as free as an eagle soaring the sky,
PLUMP now was rid of that misguided guy.
The next step was for the people to say,
"We must appoint a hero and do it today."
A hero named "Robert Moral" was appointed in haste,
And **PLUMP** soon realized the charges he faced.

Moral succeeded in proving collusion,
Tootin and **PLUMP'S** actions weren't an illusion.
In the end the people defeated and trumped,
The man who they had known as **RONALD PLUMP**.
The people rejoiced at this great resolution,
And as for our story, that's the conclusion.

Dedicated to the future of America,
our children, and the world's children.

THE END